SHORT WALKS SOUTH DOWNS:
BRIGHTON, EASTBOURNE AND ARUNDEL

by Nike Werstroh and Jacint Mig

Fantastic views of fields and low hills (Walk 4)

CONTENTS

Using this guide... 4
Route summary table 6
Map key 7
Introduction... 9
   Walking in the South Downs... 10
   Things to see 10
   Travel 11
   Where to stay... 11

The walks
1.   Arundel and River Arun 13
2.   Chanctonbury Ring.. 19
3.   Highdown Hill 25
4.   Cissbury Ring 29
5.   Bramber Castle and River Adur 33
6.   Fulking Escarpment 39
7.   Devil's Dyke 45
8.   Castle Hill 49
9.   Mount Caburn 57
10. Alfriston and Bo Peep Hill 63
11. The Long Man of Wilmington 69
12. Litlington White Horse 73
13. Seaford Head 77
14. Seven Sisters 81
15. Beachy Head 89

Useful information... 93

USING THIS GUIDE

Routes in this book

In this book you will find a selection of easy or moderate walks suitable for almost everyone, including casual walkers and families with children, or for when you only have a short time to fill. The routes have been carefully chosen to allow you to explore the area and its attractions. Most routes are circular, although some linear walks may be included that use public transport to get back to the start. Although there may be some climbs there is no challenging terrain, but do bear in mind that conditions can sometimes be wet or muddy underfoot. A route summary table is included on page 6 to help you choose the right walk.

Clothing and footwear

You won't need any special equipment to enjoy these walks. The weather in Britain can be changeable, so choose clothing suitable for the season and wear or carry a waterproof jacket. For footwear, comfortable walking boots or trainers with a good grip are best. A small rucksack for drinks, snacks and spare clothing is useful. See www.adventuresmart.uk.

Walk descriptions

At the beginning of each walk you'll find all the information you need:

- start/finish location, with postcode and a what3words address to help you find it
- parking and transport information, estimated walking time, total distance and climb
- details of public toilets available along the route and where you can get refreshments
- a summary of the key highlights of the walk and what you might see

Timings given are the time to complete the walk at a reasonable walking pace. Allow extra time for extended stops or if walking with children.

The route is described in clear, easy-to-follow directions, with each waypoint marked on an accompanying map extract. It's a good idea to read the whole of the route instructions before setting out, so that you know what to expect.

Maps, GPX files and what3words

Extracts from the OS® 1:25,000 map accompany each route. GPX files for all the walks in this book are available to download at www.cicerone.co.uk/1203/gpx.

What3words is a free smartphone app which identifies every 3m square of the globe with a unique three-word address, e.g. ///destiny.cafe.sonic. For more information see https://what3words.com/products/what3words-app.

USING THIS GUIDE

Walking with children

Even young children can be surprisingly strong walkers, but every family is different and you may need to adapt the timings given in this book to take that into account. Make sure you go at the pace of the slowest member and choose a walk with an exciting objective in mind, such as a cave, river, waterfall or picnic spot. Many of the walks can be shortened to suit – suggestions are included at the end of the route description.

Dogs

Sheep or cattle may be found grazing on a number of these walks. Keep dogs under control at all times so that they don't scare or disturb livestock or wildlife. Cattle, particularly cows with calves, may very occasionally pose a risk to walkers with dogs. If you ever feel threatened by cattle, you should let go of your dog's lead and let it run free.

Enjoying the countryside responsibly

Enjoy the countryside and treat it with respect to protect our natural environments. Stick to footpaths and take your litter home with you. When driving, slow down on rural roads and park considerately, or better still use public transport. For more details check out www.gov.uk/countryside-code.

The Countryside Code

Respect everyone
- be considerate to those living in, working in and enjoying the countryside
- leave gates and property as you find them
- do not block access to gateways or driveways when parking
- be nice, say hello, share the space
- follow local signs and keep to marked paths unless wider access is available

Protect the environment
- take your litter home – leave no trace of your visit
- do not light fires and only have BBQs where signs say you can
- always keep dogs under control and in sight
- dog poo – bag it and bin it – any public waste bin will do
- care for nature – do not cause damage or disturbance

Enjoy the outdoors
- check your route and local conditions
- plan your adventure – know what to expect and what you can do
- enjoy your visit, have fun, make a memory

SHORT WALKS SOUTH DOWNS – BRIGHTON, EASTBOURNE AND ARUNDEL

ROUTE SUMMARY TABLE

WALK NAME	START POINT	TIME	DISTANCE
1. Arundel and the River Arun	Arundel railway station	2¾hr	8km (5 miles)
2. Chanctonbury Ring	Washington	2¾hr	8km (5 miles)
3. Highdown Hill	Highdown Gardens	1¼hr	3.5km (2¼ miles)
4. Cissbury Ring	Storrington Rise car park	2hr	6km (3¾ miles)
5. Bramber Castle and the River Adur	Bramber	2¼hr	6km (3¾ miles)
6. Fulking Escarpment	Fulking	2hr	5km (3 miles)
7. Devil's Dyke	Devil's Dyke	1¾hr	4km (2½ miles)
8. Castle Hill	Castle Hill car park	3½hr	10.5km (6½ miles)
9. Mount Caburn	Glynde railway station	2½hr	9km (5½ miles)
10. Alfriston and Bo Peep Hill	Alfriston	2½hr	9km (5½ miles)
11. The Long Man of Wilmington	Priory car park, Wilmington	1½hr	4.5km (2¾ miles)
12. Litlington White Horse	Seven Sisters Country Park Visitor Centre	2¼hr	7km (4¼ miles)
13. Seaford Head	Seaford Museum	3hr	9.5km (6 miles)
14. Seven Sisters	Seven Sisters Country Park Visitor Centre	4hr	13km (8 miles)
15. Beachy Head	Eastbourne	1¾hr	4.5km (2¾ miles)

MAP KEY

HIGHLIGHTS
Castle, market town, riverside path
Iron Age hill fort, views
Views, Highdown Gardens
Iron Age hill fort, history, views
Castle ruins, history, river
Stunning chalk downland, views
Views, history
Chalk grassland, views
Iron Age hill fort, views, meadows
Chalk ridge with sea views, pretty village
Long Man chalk figure, coastal views
White Horse chalk figure, river
White cliffs, sea views, beach, river
White cliffs, sea views, meadows and forest
Sea views, lighthouse

SYMBOLS USED ON ROUTE MAPS

- **S** — Start point
- **F** — Finish point
- **SF** — Start and finish at the same place
- **4** — Waypoint
- ~ — Route line

MAPPING IS SHOWN AT A SCALE OF 1:25,000

0 KM — 0.25 — 0.5
0 miles — 0.25

DOWNLOAD THE GPX FILES FOR FREE AT
www.cicerone.co.uk/1203/GPX

Looking back towards Kingston (Walk 8)

INTRODUCTION

Iron age hill fort on top of Highdown Hill (Walk 3)

From the famous white cliffs of the south coast to the ramparts of Iron Age forts, from castle ruins to mysterious chalk figures on grassy slopes, from pretty villages to cosy traditional pubs – there is so much to explore in the South Downs.

There might not be any high hills in the South Downs, but this open landscape characterised by rolling chalk downland with dry valleys offers some surprisingly fine views. The chalk grassland is an important habitat for a variety of wildlife. However, this densely populated landscape has been used and shaped by human hands since the Stone Age. As you walk the trails, you will sooner or later stumble upon one of the many Iron Age hill forts that occupy some of the most prominent hilltops in the area.

The rolling fields surrounding the villages have been grazed by sheep for centuries and you'll find the presence of farming as you traverse fields with crops and go through countless kissing gates. But the chalky soil, proximity to the sea and the mild climate also creates good conditions for a few small vineries to produce delicious sparkling wines.

The South Downs only gained national park status in 2011, becoming one of the newest national parks in the UK. The extensive network of paths provides many routes for walkers and runners, while the narrow roads, bridleways and the chalky South Downs

SHORT WALKS SOUTH DOWNS — BRIGHTON, EASTBOURNE AND ARUNDEL

Way attract cyclists and mountain bikers in great numbers.

Day trippers have been coming to the seaside towns such as Brighton and Eastbourne since the opening of the London to Brighton railway line in the 1840s. Many of the small fishing towns became fashionable holiday hotspots with grand hotels. Writers such as Virginia Woolf and Rudyard Kipling were so inspired by the beautiful scenery of the downs that they chose to live and work here for many years.

A common type of waymarker that can be seen around the South Downs

Walking in the South Downs

Walking is by far the best way to explore the South Downs. The 15 walks in this book focus on the eastern parts of the South Downs National Park, between Arundel and Eastbourne. They can be enjoyed all year round through the changing seasons, and whether you are interested in a leisurely riverside stroll, the dramatic white cliffs of the Seven Sisters, or panoramic views you'll find a walk to suit. Many of the walks described make use of the South Downs Way, a long-distance footpath that follows old routes and traverses chalk ridges, meadows and pastures between Winchester and Eastbourne. Allow time to marvel at the far-reaching views, stop for a picnic, or finish your walk in a cosy pub in one of the charming villages.

Things to see

With a good train service from London and helpful bus links from the coastal towns, it is easy to explore the South Downs National Park. Follow the popular coastal walks from Eastbourne (Walk 15) or Seaford (Walk 14) for great views of the famous Seven Sisters cliffs. Stroll the streets of the charming town of Arundel and explore its grand castle (Walk 1), walk to Iron Age hill forts (Walks 2 and 4) or follow a section of the South Downs Way (Walks 2 and 10) on a chalk ridge with panoramic views. During WW2 Sussex became a front line of defence against invasion on the south coast, and some of the pillboxes and anti-tank obstacles can still be seen in places like Cuckmere Haven.

WHERE TO STAY

Cliffs of the Seven Sisters seen from just before the Coastguard Cottages (Walk 13)

Travel

From London there are frequent train services to Brighton, Eastbourne and Arundel, therefore many of the walks are easily accessible from the capital for a pleasant day out. The major towns can be reached by train and most of the villages mentioned in the book are served by buses. The walks in this book are all circular. A few start from a car park that might be easier to reach by your own transport or by a short taxi or Uber ride.

Where to stay

If you want to stay in the area for a couple of days there is plenty of accommodation in Brighton, Eastbourne or in other seaside towns such as Worthing or Seaford, with several options in Arundel. There are also inns and B&Bs in the villages, for example Alfriston and Bramber, or if you are after something more special there are holiday cottages available.

The imposing Hiorne Tower in Arundel Park

WALK 1
Arundel and the River Arun

Start/finish	Arundel railway station
Locate	BN18 9PH ///soonest.chucks.shirtless
Cafes/pubs	Cafes, restaurants and pubs in Arundel, tearoom by Swanbourne Lake
Transport	Trains from London
Parking	Station car park, Mill Road car park next to Arundel Museum (charges apply)
Toilets	At station and by museum building

Time 2¾hr
Distance 8km (5 miles)
Climb 80m

A stroll through a picturesque market town followed by a riverside walk with amazing views over to Arundel Castle

This walk takes you through the charming town of Arundel, its high street dotted with independent cafes, cosy pubs and fascinating antique shops. Leaving town you walk through Arundel park and then drop down to Swanbourne Lake before joining the path beside the River Arun. The return to Arundel is alongside the river with some fantastic views towards Arundel Castle. Complete your day with a visit to the restored medieval castle.

View of Arundel Castle from the river path

SHORT WALKS SOUTH DOWNS – BRIGHTON, EASTBOURNE AND ARUNDEL

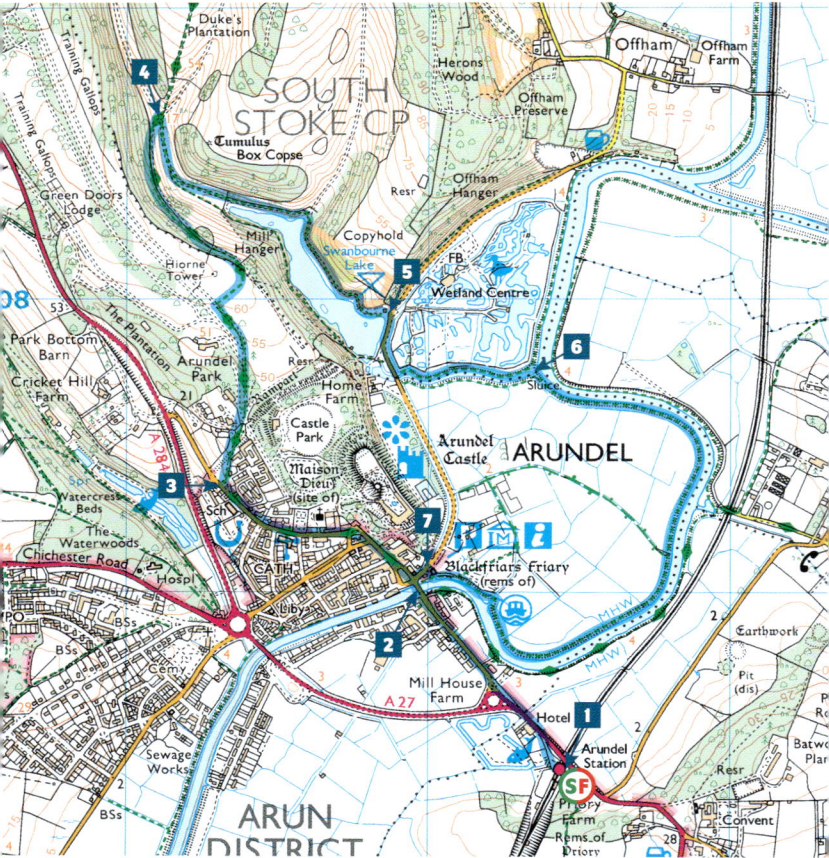

1 From Arundel train station take Station Approach and then keep left on The Causeway (A27). Cross at the pedestrian crossing just before the roundabout and then continue on The Causeway, which becomes Queen Street further on, and about 400m from the roundabout reach Arundel Bridge.

2 Cross the bridge and continue straight on along the High Street. Then

WALK 1 – ARUNDEL AND THE RIVER ARUN

St Nicholas' church was built in 1380

walk alongside the castle's wall and join London Road. Pass the 14th-century church of St Nicholas and shortly afterwards reach **Arundel Cathedral**.

> The current cathedral building was commissioned in 1868 by Henry, 15th Duke of Norfolk. Built in a French Gothic style, it was a Catholic parish church from 1873 and only became cathedral in 1965 with the foundation of the Diocese of Arundel and Brighton.

About 150m further on pass a school and keep right alongside a wall, entering **Arundel Park**.

3 Go through the gate and follow the Monarch's Way straight on, initially on the wide paved road. Leaving the paved road, go right by the signpost and follow the Monarch's Way towards **Hiorne Tower**. The tower was built in 1797 by architect Francis Hiorne in a bid for the contract to rebuild the castle. He did not succeed and the tower remains a folly. After passing the tower meet and cross a broad path and continue along the Monarch Way's straight on downhill. Shortly afterwards keep left through the kissing gate and then traverse the hillside, with views on the right. Descend the chalky path to a path junction.

Swanbourne Lake is a popular spot with visitors

4 At the junction go sharply right. Follow the wide path, ignoring any other paths. Go through the kissing gate and walk alongside **Swanbourne Lake** to arrive at Swanbourne Lodge Tea Room.

5 Go through the gate by the tea room and emerge onto **Mill Road** and turn right. Follow the road, then at the foot of the bridge go left on a path. Walk alongside the river, keeping right at the T-junction to cross a **sluice**.

6 Go through a gate and at the path junction continue straight on with the river on your left. You can enjoy some amazing views over to Arundel Castle to your right. Ignore any other paths and stay alongside the river until the path slowly bends away and then curves back towards the castle. Skirt the car park and arrive at the **Arundel Museum** building.

7 Rejoining Mill Road keep left. The entrance of the castle is almost opposite the museum. At the roundabout go left, cross the bridge and return to Arundel station.

WALK 1 – ARUNDEL AND THE RIVER ARUN

− To shorten
From Swanbourne Lake go right on Mill Road and follow it to Arundel Castle without joining the path alongside the river, saving about 1km (20min).

+ To lengthen
From Swanbourne Lake go left on Mill Road and follow it to the Black Rabbit pub. From the pub's car park take the path alongside the river back to Arundel, rejoining the main route at Waypoint 6. Allow an extra 20min.

Arundel Castle

Founded in 1067 by Roger de Montgomery, Earl of Arundel, the castle was a hereditary stately home of the Dukes of Norfolk and their ancestors for over 850 years. Some of the original features such as the Norman keep and the medieval gatehouse still remain. It was one of the first stately homes to have electricity, central heating and domestic water installed, as part of major restoration work carried out at the end of the 19th century by Henry, 15th Duke of Norfolk. The castle and its garden are open for visitors from 1 April to 29 October. For information about entrance fees and opening times visit www.arundelcastle.org.

Heading back to Arundel Castle along the River Arun

Exploring the earth works of the Iron Age hill fort

WALK 2
Chanctonbury Ring

Start/finish	*Frankland Arms pub, Washington*
Locate	*RH20 4AL ///headset.bookmark.noon*
Cafes/pubs	*Pub in Washington*
Transport	*Buses from Worthing*
Parking	*Plenty of parking places at the edge of village and along London Road*
Toilets	*No public toilets on route*

Time 2¾hr
Distance 8km (5 miles)
Climb 220m

A walk along the South Downs Way to an Iron Age hill fort

This rewarding circular walk from Washington village takes you through fields, then after a gentle ascent follows a section of the South Downs Way to Chanctonbury Ring, one of the many Iron Age hill forts in the South Downs. Impressive views of rolling fields accompany you for most of the trail.

The grassy top of Chanctonbury Hill is a great location for a rest and a picnic

SHORT WALKS SOUTH DOWNS – BRIGHTON, EASTBOURNE AND ARUNDEL

1 With the **Frankland Arms pub** on your right follow the Washington Bostal road out of the village for a short way to find a public footpath on the left.

2 Leave the road along the footpath. Cross the stream on a wooden bridge and then go up steps alongside a fence. Climb over a stile into a field and continue alongside the fence. Carry straight on by the wooden signpost. Low hills dominate the views and soon some farm buildings come into view. Go through a gate into a grazing field and by the wooden signpost keep slightly right away from the fence line and cross the field diagonally to the next gate. Cross another field and after a gate follow the path across the next field diagonally to reach the treeline and a gate. The private woodland belongs to

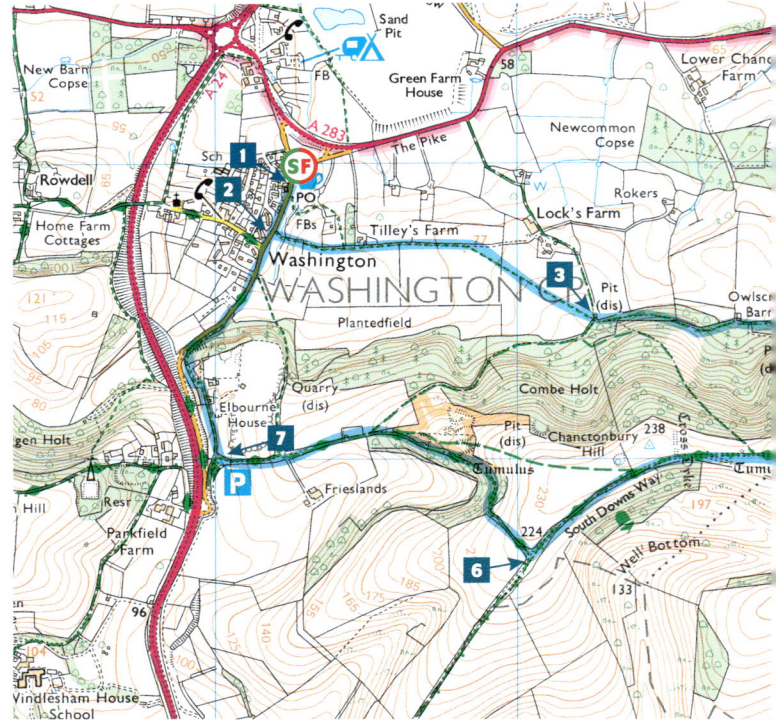

WALK 2 – CHANTONBURY RING

Wiston Estate, also known for its winery producing award-winning wines.

3 Go through the gate then keep left through the big gate. The path bends away from the fence through forest. Wild garlic and blue bells carpet the woodland floor in spring. Carry straight on, ignoring all the other paths, and cross a clearing with a ruined **barn**. About 15–20min after entering the woods pass an information board about the Wiston Estate. Emerging from the woods, pass a cottage to reach a junction.

4 Go right and then follow the public bridleway straight on with the community farm on your left. Walk towards the hill, passing the water works. Ascend the bridleway to meet the **South Downs Way** (SDW) at a junction.

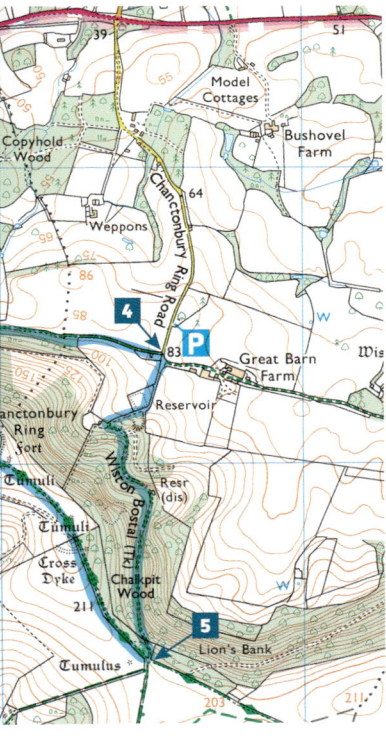

In spring wild garlic can be seen on the northern slopes of Chanctonbury Hill

The route joins the South Downs Way

5 Go right on the SDW and follow it for about 10–15min, with some great views of rolling low hills, to the tree-covered **Chanctonbury Ring**. The SDW skirts the treeline and then curves away from the ring. (Leave the SDW if you want explore the ramparts). The route continues along the chalky SDW, with some fantastic views. On the far right you can make out the hills of the North Downs and on the left the sea. Reach a junction with a wooden signpost.

6 Keep right at the junction and descend on the SDW, with further views of the North Downs in the distance. Walk through woods and then alongside grazing fields. Ignore any other bridleways and on reaching a track go right to a car park.

7 Walk across the Wiston Estate **car park** and then, leaving the SDW, keep right on the public footpath. Follow a private drive and just before reaching the house go left on the footpath through woods. Look out for some overgrown old kilns on the right-hand side of the track as you descend. Arrive at a tarmac road, keep right and, ignoring any other roads, walk back to the pub.

> **— To shorten**
>
> **Start from Wiston Estate car park and follow the South Downs Way to Chanctonbury Ring. Return the same way (4.5km or 1hr 30min there and back).**

Chanctonbury Ring

Chanctonbury Ring Iron Age hill fort

This circular earthen rampart dates back to the late Bronze or early Iron Age. It might have had a defensive purpose or have been used as a religious place. It was abandoned for centuries before it was reoccupied during the Roman period, when two Roman temples were built in the fort. In the late 4th century the site was abandoned once again and the area was used for grazing until the 18th century, when a ring of beech trees was planted around the perimeter. The trees were destroyed in the great storm of 1987 and were periodically replanted, giving an opportunity to carry out excavations on the site.

Walking along the ramparts of the fort

WALK 3
Highdown Hill

Start/finish	*Highdown Gardens, west of Worthing*
Locate	*BN12 6FB ///spark.noon.lights*
Cafes/pubs	*Pub at the start/finish*
Transport	*No public transport available*
Parking	*Car park near Highdown Gardens (take Highdown Rise from A259)*
Toilets	*In Highdown Gardens next to car park*

Time 1¼hr
Distance 3.5km (2¼ miles)
Climb 85m

A stroll through fields with some great views to the coast

This easy walk takes you to the earthwork rings of Highdown Hillfort and then alongside fields, with some great views towards the coast and the downs. It is worth spending some time exploring the beautiful Highdown Gardens after the walk, then you can treat yourself to a meal or drink in the grand building nearby – now a welcoming pub with guest rooms, it was originally built as a family house in the 1820s.

Views of rolling hills from the route

SHORT WALKS SOUTH DOWNS – BRIGHTON, EASTBOURNE AND ARUNDEL

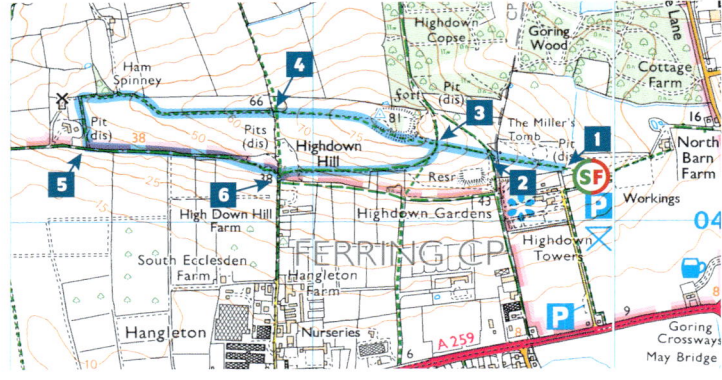

1 Leave the car park by the South Downs National Park information board, near the entrance to Highdown Gardens. Follow the well-trodden path across the meadow to **Miller's Tomb**.

> Legend has it that the Highdown miller, John Olliver, was involved in smuggling – he signalled to the vessels with the sails of the wind-mill. Curiously he also erected his own tomb nearly 30 years before he died in 1793.

2 Go through the gate and continue straight on, ignoring the path on the left. Head slightly uphill towards a signpost on the meadow, with views towards the sea on your left.

3 At the four-way bridleway junction with the signpost continue straight on. (Later you will return to this junction

Miller's Tomb

from the left.) Shortly afterwards notice the ramparts of the Iron Age **fort** on your right. Take one of several paths heading in the direction of the Highdown New Mill in the near distance, to reach a field gate. There are views towards the sea and the built-up coastline around Worthing, and soon you can also make out Arundel Castle in the distance.

WALK 3 — HIGHDOWN HILL

Walking towards Highdown New Mill, a converted windmill

4 Go through the gate and follow the path sandwiched between fields alongside a fence. The path turns sharply left, skirting around a field with the **mill tower** on your right to reach a junction.

5 Turn left along the public bridleway and follow it among bushes, with views towards Worthing, arriving at a path junction with a signpost.

6 Ignore the path with steps on the left and keep left, slightly uphill, on the next path by the National Trust plaque for **Highdown Hill**. Ignore a path on the left and continue straight on. Then keep left on the public bridleway by a signpost and arrive back at the four-way junction you passed earlier. Turn right and retrace your steps to the car park.

Highdown Gardens

Highdown Gardens started in 1909 as an experiment to see what would grow on the chalk soil. Sir Frederick Stern and Lady Sybil Stern invested in seeds and cuttings, and hired plant hunters to make collecting expeditions to China. Stern also set up a laboratory to count plant chromosomes and shared his experiences in lectures and his book *The Chalk Garden*. When Stern died in 1967 the gardens were donated to Worthing Borough Council. This unique chalk garden is free to visit. For opening times and further information about the garden's history and events visit www.highdowngardens.co.uk.

Views of the South Downs from Cissbury Ring

WALK 4
Cissbury Ring

Start/finish	*Storrington Rise car park, Findon Valley*
Locate	*BN14 0HT ///highly.heartache.pills*
Cafes/pubs	*None on route*
Transport	*Buses from Worthing to Findon Valley (stops on A24 road, about 300m from the car park)*
Parking	*Storrington Rise car park (located at the edge of Findon Valley off the A24)*
Toilets	*No public toilets on route*

Time 2hr
Distance 6km (3¾ miles)
Climb 190m

Explore the largest hill fort in Sussex with panoramic views to the coastline

There is a network of paths and numerous ways to explore the earthwork ring of this Iron Age fort. The walk described here first skirts below the ring, allowing you to enjoy the views towards the north, and then climbs to the ramparts and follows them anticlockwise, with further views of the South Downs and towards the coastline.

Steps lead up to the ramparts of the fort

SHORT WALKS SOUTH DOWNS – BRIGHTON, EASTBOURNE AND ARUNDEL

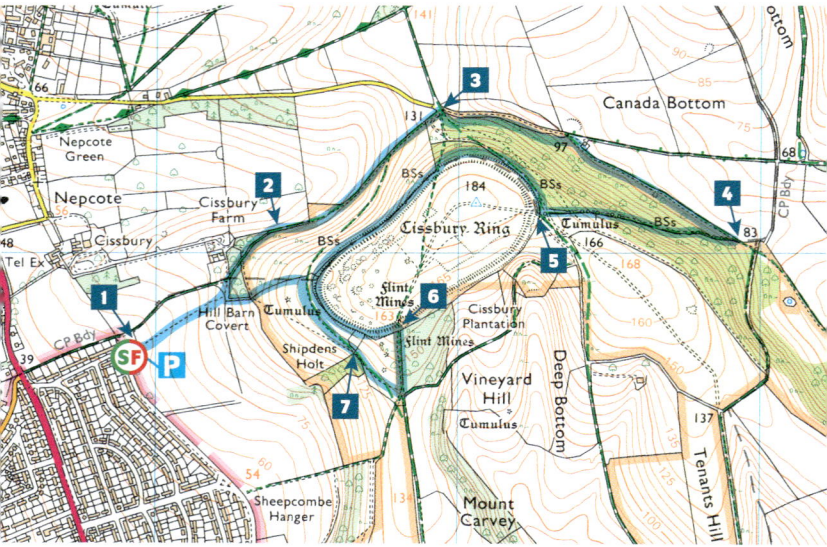

1 From the car park take the path uphill towards the treeline, keeping slightly left (there are several other paths crossing the hillside). Enter the woods by the fence and keep right uphill, following the well-trodden path alongside the fence. Ignore gates on both sides and follow the path between fences to a farm gate.

2 Go through the gate and continue along the public bridleway. Walk alongside fields with **Cissbury Ring** slightly above on your right. Go through a gate and reach a track. Walk to the wooden signpost and locate a National Trust sign.

3 Keep right on a path by the National Trust sign just before the gate. Shortly afterwards keep left slightly downhill and follow the path parallel to a track, with some fine views of rolling fields on the left. Pass a barn and come to a junction.

4 At the junction (just before the gate) go sharply right uphill. Ignore any joining paths and locate the next wooden public bridleway marker near the track. Cross the track, go through a kissing gate and climb the chalky path. Shortly afterwards reach **Cissbury Ring**.

WALK 4 – CISSBURY RING

The route goes alongside fields with Cissbury Ring above on the right

5 Steps lead to the ramparts on both sides; go up the steps on the right. Follow the path along the ramparts anticlockwise, with some fantastic views of fields and low hills. Ignore the steps going down to the path you walked along below the ramparts. Soon the coastline comes into view. Ignore another set of steps going down to the lower path and continue along the ramparts until you reach a gap. There are two sets of steps here just like where you joined the path onto the ramparts.

The first archaeological dig on Cissbury Ring took place in 1857. Further investigations carried out by the Victorians confirmed the existence of a Neolithic flint mine.

6 Go down the steps and keep right in the gap. Descend away from the ramparts through trees and then through a kissing gate. Keep right at a clearing by the signpost (just before the field gate) and descend to a wooden gate.

7 Go through the gate to a grassy area and keep parallel to the fence, with some views towards the sea (on your left). Keep left just before you reach the next gate, and continue with the fence on your right. Drop down to a kissing gate near the trees, descend alongside the treeline and then walk across the meadow straight down to the car park.

SHORT WALKS SOUTH DOWNS – BRIGHTON, EASTBOURNE AND ARUNDEL

▬ To shorten
For a slightly shorter walk, at Waypoint 3 after the National Trust sign keep right uphill towards the steps leading up to the ramparts of Cissbury Ring. This shortens the walk by about 1.5km (30min).

Cissbury Ring

Far-reaching views to the coast from Cissbury Ring

During the Neolithic period flint mining took place in this area. Cissbury Ring was used as a burial site during the Bronze Age. The fort was built around 400BC and used for defence for about 300 years. There was also a Roman settlement on the site, with up to 11 buildings. In the Tudor period, Cissbury was part of a warning system of beacons along the south coast. From there it was possible to monitor 78 miles of coastline. During WW2 anti-aircraft guns were positioned on the hill, and the area was used for military exercises. For more information see www.nationaltrust.org.uk/visit/sussex/cissbury-ring.

WALK 5
Bramber Castle and the River Adur

Start/finish	The Street, Bramber
Locate	BN44 3WE ///instead.intervene.meatball
Cafes/pubs	Pubs and restaurant in Bramber and Upper Beeding
Transport	Buses from Shoreham, Worthing
Parking	Car park on The Street and small car park near castle (charges apply)
Toilets	In car park on The Street

Time 2¼hr
Distance 6km (3¾ miles)
Climb 40m

Fascinating castle ruins and a mostly level riverside walk

This delightful route takes you from the ruins of Bramber Castle along the snaking River Adur. The meadow with the remains of Bramber Castle dotted around is a perfect spot for a summer picnic before or after your walk. To complete your day, visit St Mary's House, a medieval house with fine interiors and beautiful gardens.

Arriving in Upper Beeding alongside the River Adur

SHORT WALKS SOUTH DOWNS – BRIGHTON, EASTBOURNE AND ARUNDEL

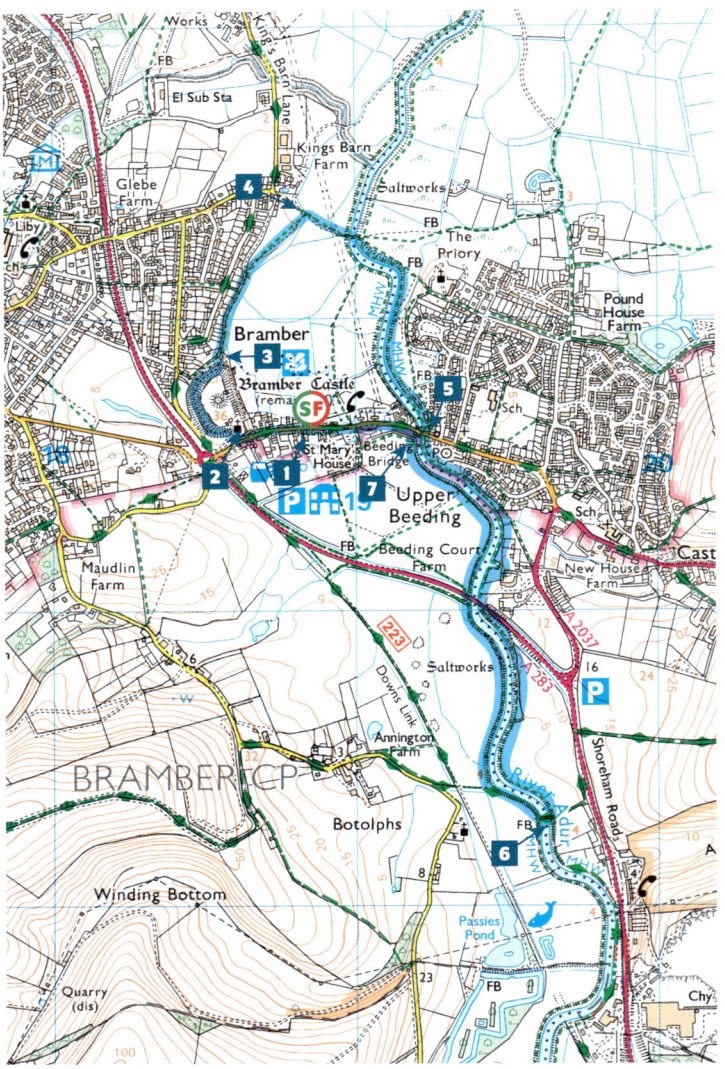

WALK 5 – BRAMBER CASTLE AND THE RIVER ADUR

St Nicholas Church by Bramber Castle

1 With the car park and bus stop on your right follow The Street and take the path on the right. Go up the steps by the Old School House, passing **St Nicholas Church** and its small churchyard.

> Originally a monastic chapel for the castle, St Nicholas became a parish church in the 13th century. The nave with its Norman doorway survives from the original building; the tower, however, dates from the 18th century.

Cross the moat, ignoring other paths, and climb the steps to arrive on a big grassy meadow with the remains of **Bramber Castle**.

2 After exploring the ruins return to and descend the steps, then take the path on the right opposite the church, by the National Trust Bramber Castle sign. Walk through woods, ignoring other paths, with the moat on your right. The path drops down, curving away from the moat and the ruins to reach a footpath.

3 Keep right on the public footpath by the fence and descend through bushes. Soon you'll get your first glimpse of the River Adur. Pass some houses and continue straight on through a kissing gate. Walk across the meadow, with the houses and gardens on your left. The path curves slightly right away from the buildings to meet another public footpath by a field gate near a stream.

Not much remains today of Bramber Castle

WALK 5 – BRAMBER CASTLE AND THE RIVER ADUR

4 Turn right, crossing the stream by a bridge. As you walk across the meadow there are views of the castle tower in the near distance. Cross the **River Adur** by a bridge and at the path junction go right, with the river on your right.

> Soon after you join the river path look out for a path on the left that leads to nearby St Peter's church. While some parts of the building date back to the 12th century it has been drastically altered in later centuries.

Continue alongside the river, going through some kissing gates to arrive at a road (The Street).

5 Cross over The Street by the bridge at **Upper Beeding** and go through a gate to continue on the footpath alongside the river. Pass a pub and its garden. When the path splits keep right closer to the river. Follow the footpath, passing under a road bridge and then alongside the river for about 15–20min to reach a footbridge.

> ⓘ *Officially opened in 1972, the South Downs Way is now the only long-distance trail that runs entirely within a national park.*

6 Joining the **South Downs Way** (SDW) go right across the bridge, and then right again. At a path junction

Wildflowers cover the riverside in spring

where the Downs Link and the SDW leave to the left, stay on the path alongside the river. Pass under the road bridge again and ignore any other paths to arrive at The Street by the bridge that connects Bramber and Upper Beeding.

7 Turn left and follow The Street to **Bramber**. Pass **St Mary's House** and its garden and walk back to the starting point. St Mary's was built around 1470 as an inn for pilgrims. For opening times check www.stmarysbramber.co.uk.

> **– To shorten**
>
> When you reach the bridge at Upper Beeding turn right across the bridge and follow The Street back to Bramber. This shortens the walk by 3km (45min).

St Mary's House was built in the 15th century

Bramber Castle

After the Norman Conquest Bramber became one of the six administrative regions of Sussex, and in 1073 a castle was built to control the area by William de Braose. The castle belonged to his descendants until 1450, when it was passed down to the Mowbray family. Large-scale subsidence ruined the castle during the 16th century, and the stones were taken for building houses and a bridge, so very little remains of the original structure. The ruins are free to visit, but there is a £2 parking fee if you want to park at the small car park near the church and are not an English Heritage member.

WALK 6
Fulking Escarpment

Start/finish	*Shepherd and Dog pub, Fulking*
Locate	*BN5 9LU ///endlessly.stint.roving*
Cafes/pubs	*Pub in Fulking*
Transport	*No public transport available*
Parking	*Free roadside parking near the pub*
Toilets	*No public toilets on route*

Time 2hr
Distance 5km (3 miles)
Climb 265m

A pleasant walk with a short steep climb and amazing views of chalk downlands

Climb the steep Fulking Escarpment, on the north side of the South Downs, to follow the South Downs Way along the chalky ridge. There's no shortage of wonderful views of the escarpment and open chalk downland as you descend back to the village. This area has provided fertile land for centuries, and agriculture, especially grazing, is still dominant.

Following the broad chalky South Downs Way

SHORT WALKS SOUTH DOWNS – BRIGHTON, EASTBOURNE AND ARUNDEL

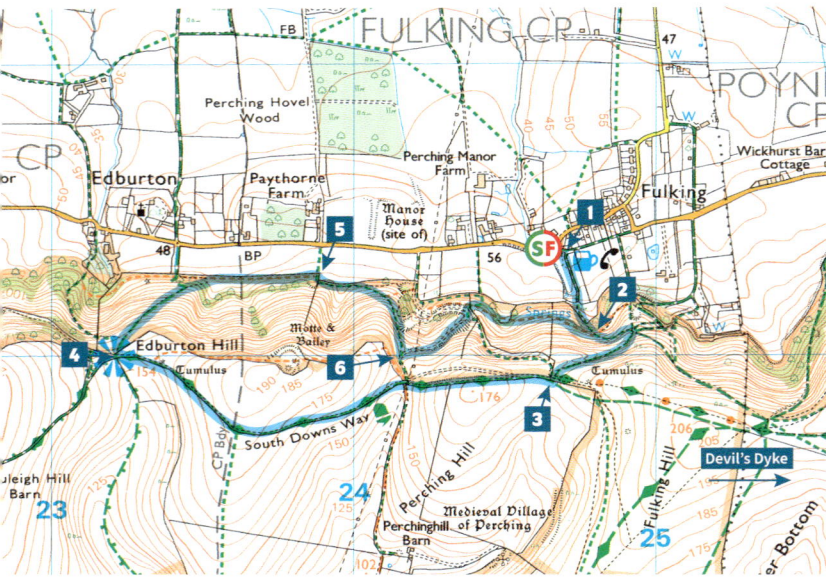

1 With the **Shepherd and Dog pub** on your right, follow Edburton Road and just after the pub building go right. Shortly afterwards turn right up the steps and follow the public footpath alongside the fence. Go over a stile and up some steps through trees to arrive at a path junction near the National Trust sign for Fulking Escarpment.

> ⓘ *Starting from Winchester, the South Downs Way long-distance trail traverses the chalk escarpment and ridges of the South Downs to Eastbourne.*

2 Continue straight on uphill. (You will return to this junction later from the right.) Ascend – ignoring a path on the left – with views of the houses of Fulking down below. You can also spot the building of the Devil's Dyke pub on the nearby hill. Come to a junction with multiple signs. Take a sharp right along a public bridleway to reach the **South Downs Way** (SDW).

3 Turn right through a gate. Follow the broad, chalky SDW alongside a fence with some excellent views of the downlands. Ignore a path on the right near an electricity pylon and go through a gate to continue on the

WALK 6 – FULKING ESCARPMENT

Great views to the north above Edburton

SDW alongside fields to a junction on **Edburton Hill**.

4 At the junction go through the gate and then immediately turn right onto the public bridleway, leaving the SDW. Go through another gate and descend the grassy path, with views towards Edburton village and beyond. Follow the most prominent path, ignoring any other paths, including a public footpath on the left. Carry straight on at a wooden signpost then walk alongside a bushy boundary (ignore a path on the left heading to the road). Pass a water trough, then go over a stile and through woods.

5 After passing another trough the path bends slightly right uphill. Head towards the electricity pylon, with views towards the village on the left. In a short while you will reach a chalky track.

6 Go left down the track, which curves left, then take the path by a stile slightly above the track on the right. After the stile descend through trees. At the path junction turn right, pass a water trough (ignore an unmarked path on the left) and shortly afterwards reach the path junction by the National Trust sign for Fulking Escarpment. Turn left and retrace your steps to the pub.

SHORT WALKS SOUTH DOWNS – BRIGHTON, EASTBOURNE AND ARUNDEL

The steep hillside of the Fulking Escarpment

– To shorten

Take a path on the right by the electricity pylon just before a gate at Waypoint 3. Rejoin the described trail at Waypoint 6, turning right along the chalky track. This shortens the walk by about 2km (40min).

+ To lengthen

On reaching the South Downs Way go left to make a detour to Devil's Dyke and back. This will add 3km to the route (allow at least an extra hour for the detour). See Walk 7 for map.

Water supply system

Located near the pub there is a hydraulic ram pump. It pumped water from Fulking Hill to a reservoir at the western edge of the street. From there, with the help of gravity, the water was led to further reservoirs, supplying two hand pumps on the street. The planning and instigating of the system are credited to the writer and philosopher John Ruskin and Henry Willet, a wealthy brewer from Brighton. From 1886 this system supplied the hamlet with piped water, until 1951 when it was replaced with mains water.

19th-century pump house by the Shepherd and Dog pub

Devil's Dyke is one of the best-known landmarks in the South Downs

WALK 7
Devil's Dyke

Start/finish	*Devil's Dyke*
Locate	*BN1 8YL ///bother.sway.years*
Cafes/pubs	*Pub at Devil's Dyke and in Poynings*
Transport	*Buses from Brighton*
Parking	*Devil's Dyke car park (from A27 take Devil's Dyke Road)*
Toilets	*At start*

Time 1¾hr
Distance 4km (2½ miles)
Climb 170m

Explore the UK's longest, deepest, widest 'dry valley'

The excellent views from Devil's Dyke have attracted people for centuries. According to legend the valley was dug by the Devil, who wanted to drown the people of the Weald. The hermit Cuthman of Steyning made a deal with the Devil: if he completed the trench in a single night he could have Cuthman's soul, but if he failed he would leave the people in peace. Fortunately, the Devil couldn't finish his evil work and the people were spared. This walk follows the rim of the valley and then drops down to the village of Poynings before climbing back up to the rim.

The Devil's Dyke pub at the start of the walk

Great views of the Weald near the start

1 Follow the road that skirts around the pub building and through the car park. From the viewpoint enjoy some excellent views of Fulking, the Weald and all the way to the North Downs. At the end of the car park continue straight on along the public footpath. There are two parallel paths; follow the public footpath and shortly the chalky path merges from the left. Crossing another path descend straight on, with views of rolling hills. Ignoring a path on the right drop down to a chalky path.

> The Devil's Dyke was briefly used as a bomb testing site during WW1. The bombs were suspended from cables from the pylons located on the side of the valley.

2 Go left through the gate and continue on the public bridleway, going straight on by the wooden signpost and ignoring the public footpath on the left. Go through a gate and descend on a path fringed with trees, ignoring a path on the right. At the next path junction follow the path marked with purple arrows downhill through woods to reach a path junction.

3 At the junction keep right alongside the fence and head towards the houses. Follow the paved Dyke Lane past houses into **Poynings** and when you reach Poynings Road turn right, pass a pub (the Royal Oak) and follow the road for about 100m to a garage.

4 Leave the road to the right, walk across the garage's yard and continue along the public footpath by a stream. Cross a bridge with a reservoir on the right. Walk alongside a fence and at a

WALK 7 – DEVIL'S DYKE

path junction go right through shrubs. Continue straight on along the public bridleway. The path crosses over the stream. Ignore any public footpaths on the left and continue on the public bridleway, going straight on at each junction until you come to a gate.

5 Go through the gate and then keep slightly left by the National Trust Devil's Dyke sign. Climbing the wide path, ignore a path on the left. Keep left uphill by the bench and signpost and then left again on the bridleway to meet the **South Downs Way** (SDW) by a signpost.

6 Turn right and follow the SDW, ignoring any other paths, to reach a road. Turn right and follow the road back to the car park.

Views across the valley of Devil's Dyke

– To shorten

On reaching the chalky path at Waypoint 2 turn right and follow it to the small play area (located close the car park) dedicated to the Victorian adventure park. This will cut the total distance down to 2km (45min).

Devil's Dyke in the Victorian era

Thanks to the fantastic views and its proximity to Brighton, Devil's Dyke became a popular destination during the Victorian era. In 1887 a railway link was built to bring people to admire the unique landscape. Then, in 1892, when H J Hubbart – traveller and game hunter – bought Dyke Estate, he turned the area into an adventure park. Merry-go-rounds, bicycle railways and funfair rides attracted visitors, and in 1894 Britain's first aerial cable car started to operate across the 300m wide valley. From 1897 people could also take the Steep Grade Railway down to Poynings. The Brighton–Dyke railway was closed in 1938, and today the old line is used as a cycle path. For more information visit www.nationaltrust.org.uk/visit/sussex/devils-dyke.

WALK 8
Castle Hill

Start/finish	*Castle Hill car park*
Locate	*BN2 6NT ///magically.kilt.hounded*
Cafes/pubs	*Pub in Kingston, restaurant and pub in Woodingdean*
Transport	*Buses from Brighton*
Parking	*Castle Hill car park, on B2123 road outside Woodingdean*
Toilets	*No public toilets on route*

Time 3½hr
Distance 10.5km (6½ miles)
Climb 315m

A moderate walk over rolling chalk grassland then a steep climb with sea views

This delightful circular route offers some open views as it traverses the grassy downland and drops down to Kingston. From the village there is a steep climb with views towards the sea. The Castle Hill Nature Reserve has protected the ancient grassland and its wildlife since 1975 and the surrounding area has been grazed for centuries. Take a picnic to make it a day out or seek out the pub in Kingston for a pit stop.

Descending on the chalky path towards Kingston

The path cuts through fields of crops near the Castle Hill Nature Reserve

WALK 8 – CASTLE HILL

Magnificent scenery surrounds the village of Kingston-near-Lewis

1 Facing the two paths with barriers, take the path on the left. Go through the barrier and follow this restricted byway away from the B2123 road. Walk alongside fields and pass a radio antenna just before **Newmarket Hill**. Rolling fields dominate the views as you follow the path between fences. Come to a junction where a public bridleway crosses the restricted byway.

2 Continue straight on at the junction. (You will return to this junction later from the right.) A short way further on the South Downs Way (SDW) joins from the left. Follow the SDW straight on through the gate and along **Juggs Road**. This ancient ridgeway was named after the Brighton fishwives who transported fish in baskets and earthenware jugs for the market in Lewes. There are rolling fields as far as you can see as you climb slightly alongside the fence as far as a gate.

3 Go through the gate and take the path on the left downhill towards **Kingston**, leaving the SDW which continues to the right. Descend the chalky path alongside the fence. Keep left on the restricted byway towards houses.

4 At the junction by the first house keep right along a path. Reach Church Lane and continue straight on, passing houses and ignoring any other roads. The lane becomes a path as you pass a football field, tennis court and picnic area. Keep right on the bridleway with the 13th-century **St Pancras Church** on the left.

SHORT WALKS SOUTH DOWNS – BRIGHTON, EASTBOURNE AND ARUNDEL

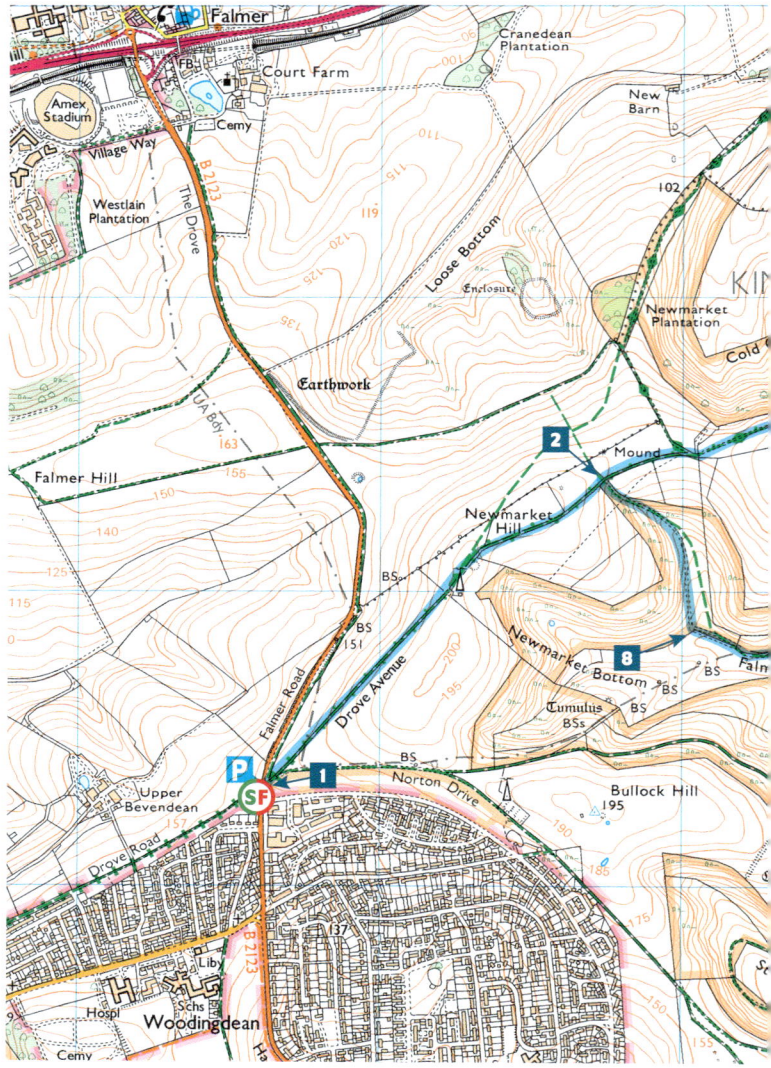

WALK 8 – CASTLE HILL

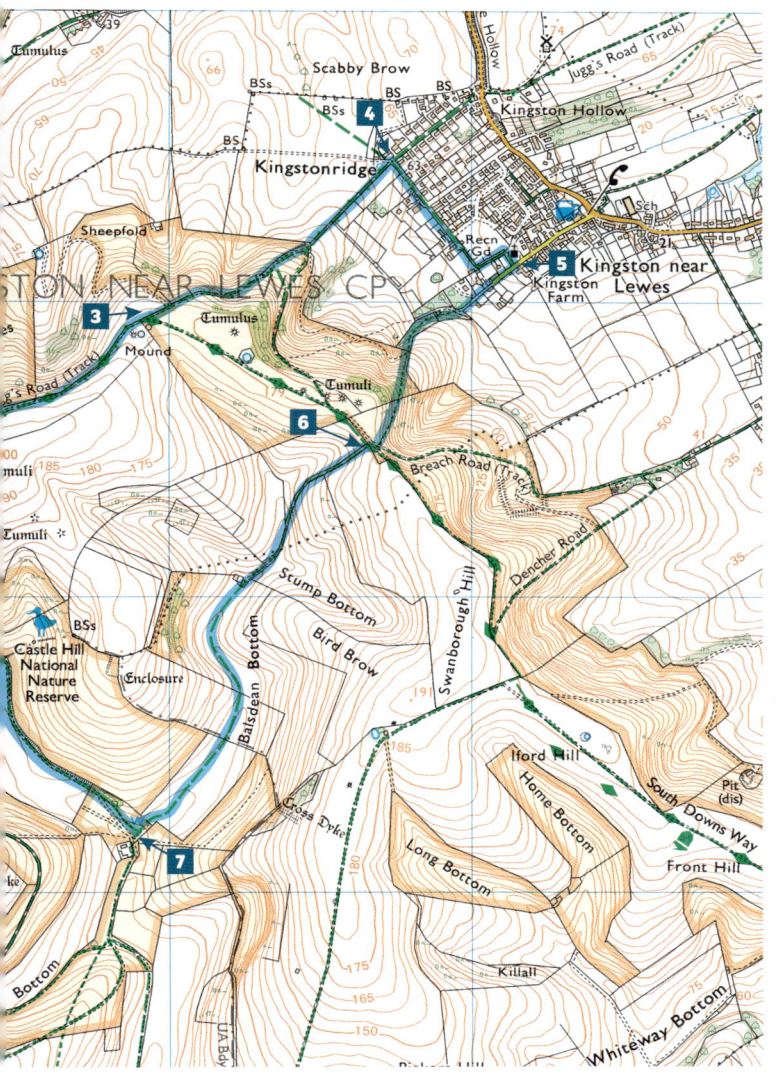

53

SHORT WALKS SOUTH DOWNS – BRIGHTON, EASTBOURNE AND ARUNDEL

Abandoned farm buildings at Falmer Bottom

5 Arrive on The Street and turn right. Turn left for 200m for the pub. Follow the road as it narrows into a path by the last house. Go through a kissing gate into woods. Ignore the path on the left and continue slightly uphill. Emerging from the woods, cross another path and carry straight on uphill. Cross two stiles and the path continues along the hillside, with fields leading the eye to the sea. Keep right on the wide path (Breach Road) and shortly after meet the SDW.

6 Cross the SDW to the signpost and cattle grid. Go over the cattle grid and descend on the public bridleway, surrounded by rolling hills. Pass a pen and after the gate carry straight on into a shallow snaking valley. Go through a gate near a water trough and cross another field to the next gate. Go across the field towards the barn and go through a gate.

> ⓘ *Up to 40 different species of wildflower and over 20 different species of butterfly can be found within just 1 square metre of the chalk grassland.*

WALK 8 – CASTLE HILL

7 Keep right near the barn buildings at **Falmer Bottom**. Follow the path along the right-hand side of a small valley. Go through another gate and continue alongside fields, with a fence on your left. Reach a gate by the board for **Castle Hill National Nature Reserve**.

8 Go through the gate and continue straight on, slightly uphill, with the fence line behind you. Climb the wide path and arrive back on the restricted byway. Turn left and retrace your steps to the car park.

> **– To shorten**
>
> At Waypoint 3 continue along the South Downs Way without going down to Kingston. After about 900m turn right to leave the SDW, rejoining the route described at Waypoint 6. This shortens the walk by 2km (45min).

Castle Hill National Nature Reserve

Common spotted orchid is one of the easiest to spot

The ancient chalk grassland within the South Downs National Park has been a designated national nature reserve since 1975. The area is rich in orchids: you can spot the rare early spider orchid as well as the common spotted and pyramidal orchid. Typical chalk flowers, such as the kidney vetch, horseshoe vetch and fairy flax, thrive in the grassland. This is also an important habitat for a wide variety of grasshoppers and crickets, and 31 of the UK's 58 species of butterflies – including the Adonis blue and chalkhill blue – have been recorded here.

On the short climb to the top of Mount Caburn

WALK 9
Mount Caburn

Start/finish	*Glynde railway station*
Locate	*BN8 6RU ///spreading.ordeals.progress*
Cafes/pubs	*Tea room and pub in Glynde*
Transport	*Trains from Brighton and Eastbourne*
Parking	*Car park on Lacy's Hill*
Toilets	*At start next to playground*

Time 2½hr
Distance 9km (5½ miles)
Climb 305m

A pleasant walk up to the site of an Iron Age hill fort and panoramic views

From the tranquil village of Glynde climb gradually to Mount Caburn, the site of an Iron Age hill fort with panoramic views. From the hilltop the route drops down to Oxteddle Bottom, then climbs from the valley and crosses meadows grazed by sheep before returning to Glynde.

Views towards the coast and the River Ouse from Mount Caburn

SHORT WALKS SOUTH DOWNS – BRIGHTON, EASTBOURNE AND ARUNDEL

1 From the train station take Lacy's Hill, crossing over the river **Glynde Reach**. Pass a car park and playground and turn left on Ranscombe Lane until you come to the post office.

2 After the post office turn right through a gate onto a public footpath. Cross a field and after a kissing gate walk up a meadow with open views for about 10–15min to a path junction by a fence.

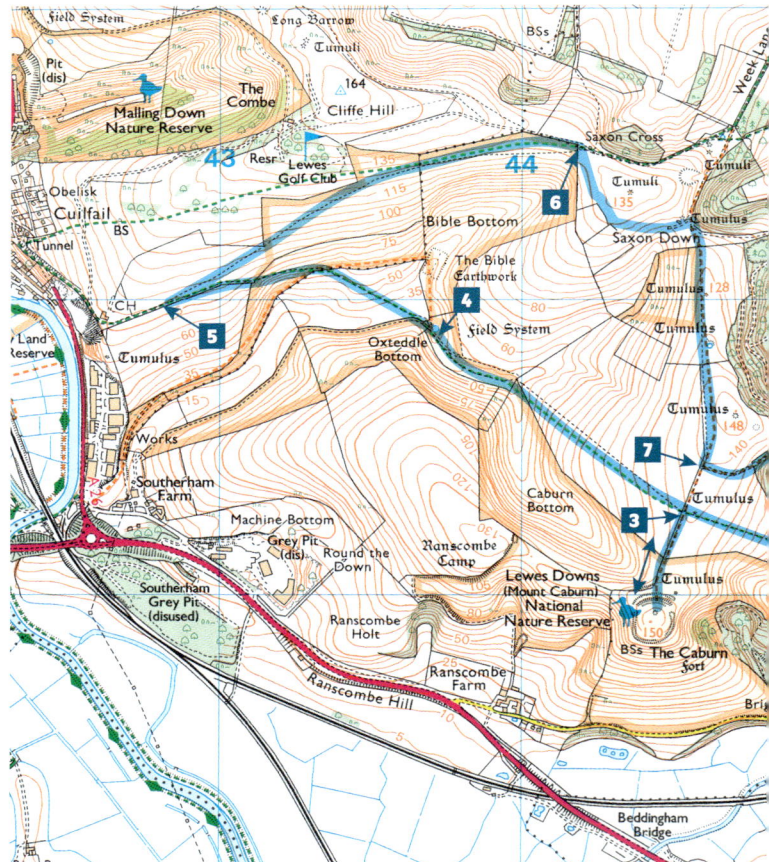

WALK 9 – MOUNT CABURN

3 Without going through the kissing gate, go left alongside the fence and shortly afterwards enter the **Mount Caburn National Nature Reserve**. Follow the narrow path crossing the moat and rampart to the top of Mount Caburn. In spring Burnt Orchids can be spotted here.

The summit of Mount Caburn was the site of an Iron Age hill fort. Locate the bench that is well positioned to enjoy the best views of the winding River Ouse and the coastline, as well as towards Lewes, Beddingham and Kingston.

Return to the path junction and go left through the kissing gate. Crossing a meadow descend for about 10min to a dry valley known as **Oxteddle Bottom**.

4 Pass a reservoir and go through a gate, then walk across the meadow diagonally uphill. Go through further gates until you meet another path near the **golf course** (Lewes Golf Club).

5 Turn right. The open views are filled with rolling hills – you can easily identify Mount Caburn in the near distance and the reservoir that is now down below on your right. Traverse the hillside above **Bible Bottom** to a gate.

6 Go through the gate by the Southerham Farm information board and keep right. Descend slightly and crossing another path go up to the field gate with a stile. After the stile cross a grazing field, climb another stile and walk alongside a fence. Reach a path junction with a gate on your right.

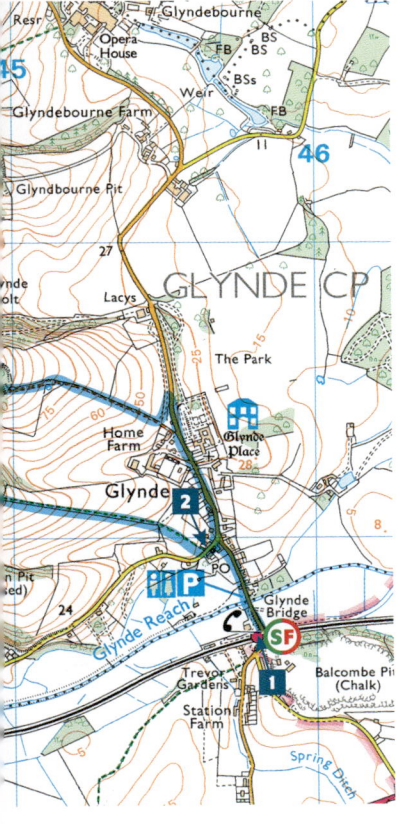

A long grassy stretch heading towards Mount Caburn

Southerham Farm Nature Reserve and the nearby Caburn Nature Reserve are home to a large number of wildflowers and some rare orchids, as well as downland butterflies such as the Adonis blue and chalkhill blue.

7 Go left and descend, first crossing a field to a kissing gate and then on a path fringed with trees and shrubs to reach the road. Turn right and follow the road back to the station (about 10min), passing **St Mary's Church**.

Palladian-style St Mary's was built on the site of a medieval church in 1765 by the bishop, Richard Trevor, next to Glynde Place, which was owned by his family.

St Mary's Church in Glynde

Looking down to Oxteddle Bottom

▬ To shorten
Returning from Mount Caburn, at the path junction continue straight on for about 100m and at Waypoint 7 turn right to return to Glynde. This makes the walk about 4km (1–1hr 30min).

Mount Caburn

By the mid Iron Age (circa 400BC) the summit of Mount Caburn was enclosed with a deep ditch and a bank of soil. Several excavations were carried out at the site between 1887 and 1998, and over 140 burial pits were found with human and animal bones and artefacts. This suggests that the enclosure might have been a religious place rather than a defensive hill fort. The area was grazed during the Roman era and then again after the Norman Conquest. In later centuries sheep grazing became the main agricultural activity. During WW2 trenches and some gun positions were dug as part of the defence line against invasion.

Weathered South Downs Way marker

WALK 10
Alfriston and Bo Peep Hill

Start/finish	*Flint Tower, Sloe Lane car park, Alfriston*
Locate	*BN26 5UP ///scraper.amphibian.saddens*
Cafes/pubs	*Pubs in Alfriston*
Transport	*Buses from Seaford and Eastbourne*
Parking	*Sloe Lane Parking (free up to 3hr), or the Willows pay-and-display car park*
Toilets	*At Sloe Lane car park*

Time 2½hr
Distance 9km (5½ miles)
Climb 260m

A gentle stroll through fields and a traverse on a chalk ridge with lovely views to the sea

This easy walk starts and ends in the charming village of Alfriston, where you can find the first property to be owned by the National Trust. Leaving the village, the route first follows a track through fields where in the summer crops dance in the constant wind. You then have a short steep climb up to join the South Downs Way along the chalk ridge to return to Alfriston, with extensive views of the Weald and towards the sea.

Views towards the coast from the South Downs Way

SHORT WALKS SOUTH DOWNS – BRIGHTON, EASTBOURNE AND ARUNDEL

WALK 10 – ALFRISTON AND BO PEEP HILL

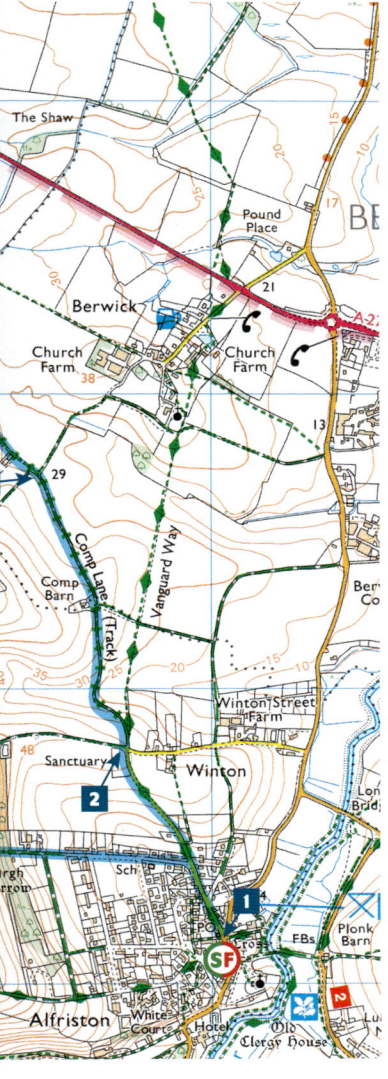

1 Start from the **Flint Tower**. *The tower was built as a playhouse in the early 20th century.* Leaving the car park, keep right on West Street and follow it to Winton Street.

2 Cross Winton Street and continue straight on along the public byway. For a few metres the public byway runs along the Vanguard Way and Cuckmere Pilgrim Way. Stay on the public byway towards a **barn** building. After the building continue straight on, slightly downhill, on a path fringed with shrubs until you reach a track.

> ⓘ *Established in 1981 by the Vanguard Rambling Club, the Vanguard Way follows paths and bridleways through peaceful villages from East Croydon to Newhaven.*

3 Go left, passing a farm. Follow the gravel track through fields to a three-way junction with a bench and continue along the track as it curves slightly left. After about 300m it meets a narrow tarmac lane.

4 Cross the lane by **Bo Peep Farm** and carry straight on along the gravel track through fields, with the ridge on your left. Pass a building (Hunter Gather Cook) and, leaving the track, keep left on a path. Walk through

The steep ascent to join the South Downs Way on the ridge

bushes for a few minutes to reach a field gate, then go up the steep hillside to the next gate.

5 Go through the gate to meet the South Downs Way (SDW) on the ridge and go left. With views over to the sea on your right, follow the SDW and soon pass **Bo Peep car park**. Walk alongside grazing fields with open views, going through some gates, for about 30min until you reach a track.

> Just a few metres to the right is Long Burg. Some 6000 years ago the Neolithic people buried their dead in long barrows (communal tombs) on the chalk hills of South Downs. Long Burg is one of the largest long barrows in Sussex.

> ⓘ *There are plenty of opportunities to observe the starry skies in the South Downs National Park, which gained Dark Sky Reserve status in 2016.*

6 At this junction the SDW continues straight on. Instead turn left along the public bridleway. Look out for a narrow path on the right. Take that path down through bushes to the houses. On reaching a street (North Road) in **Alfriston**, carry straight on to West Street where you turn right and walk back to the car park.

WALK 10 – ALFRISTON AND BO PEEP HILL

Approaching Bo Peep car park

➖ To shorten

Go left on the narrow tarmac lane by Bo Peep Farm and reach the South Downs Way at the Bo Peep car park. This shortens the walk by 1.5km (25min).

➕ To lengthen

On reaching the South Downs Way on the ridge (Waypoint 5) turn right to make a detour to Firle Beacon and back. This will add 1.5km (about 30min) to the route.

Alfriston village

Founded in the Saxon period, Alfriston is one of the oldest villages in the county. The thatched half-timbered Clerk House dates from the 14th century and was the first property acquired by the National Trust in 1896. There are several timber-framed historical inns on the High Street. The Market Cross was a famous smuggler's haunt in the 18th century. Built by the monks of Battle Abbey, The Star dates back to 1345 and was a stopover for pilgrims on their way to Chichester. The foundation of The George Inn dates to 1250 and it has been operating as a pub since 1397.

The Long Man is the largest chalk figure depicting a human in Britain

WALK 11
The Long Man of Wilmington

Start/finish	*Long Man and Priory car park, near Wilmington*
Locate	*BN26 5SW ///elbow.hiding.tips*
Cafes/pubs	*Tea room and pub in Wilmington (about 600m off route)*
Transport	*Buses from Brighton and Seaford to Wilmington*
Parking	*Long Man and Priory car park*
Toilets	*No public toilets on route*

Time 1½hr
Distance 4.5km (2¾ miles)
Climb 175m

Sweeping views of endless meadows and Britain's largest chalk figure of a human

Without a doubt the highlight of this short walk is the enormous chalk figure of the Long Man on Windower Hill. The route described then takes you above the Long Man, with sweeping views of endless meadows and the coastline, before returning to the edge of Wilmington. Don't miss the magnificent 1600-year-old yew tree in St Mary's churchyard.

The Wilmington Yew

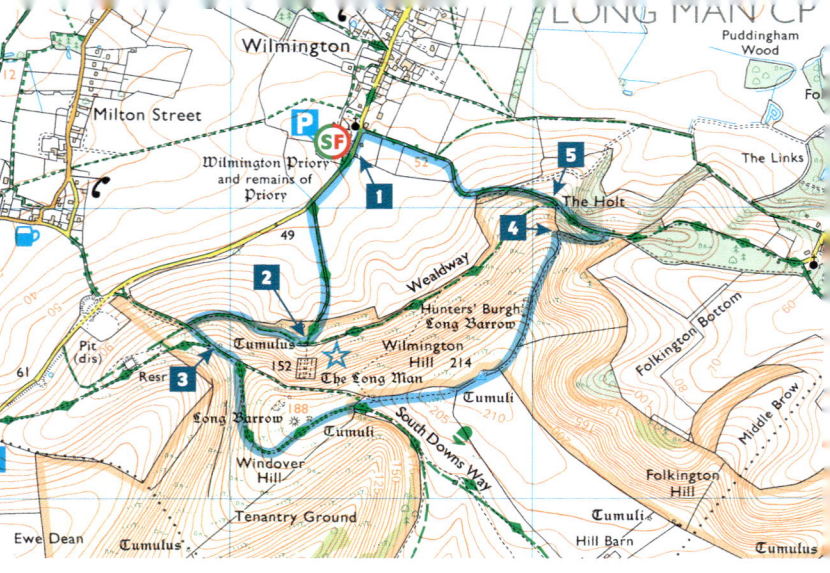

1 From the car park turn right along the tarmac lane with some views of the chalk figure on the hillside. Leave this lane to the left on a public bridleway that heads towards the **Long Man**. Walk through a field, go through a gate and, ignoring other paths, arrive at the information board just below the chalk figure.

2 Keep right with the fence on your right. Go through a gate, keep left uphill alongside the fence and shortly afterwards meet the **South Downs Way** (SDW).

3 Join the SDW, which bends slightly right away from the fence line. Rolling fields lead the eye all the way to the coastline. Go through a gate and keep slightly left alongside a fence (the SDW continues to the right). There are views of Arlington Reservoir on the left and a deep valley on the right. Pass a trig point on **Wilmington Hill**, with views towards the sea. Go through further field gates alongside a fence and descend on the grassy path.

4 When the path bends sharply right (to the left there is a stile), follow that narrow path through trees and shrubs. Go through a gate to meet a chalky path (**Wealdway**) and turn left along it for a short way to a junction.

5 At the junction continue straight on along the restricted byway (the Wealdway continues to the left). Reach a road by the cottages opposite

WALK 11 — THE LONG MAN OF WILMINGTON

At the chalk figure keep right to reach the South Downs Way

Saint Mary and Saint Peter's Church, with an ancient yew tree in the churchyard. Go left and follow the lane back to the car park.

> St Mary's Church was founded in the late 11th century to serve people in the rural area. It was also the church for the monks of Wilmington Priory. The building was modified over the centuries.

— To shorten

From the information board located at the foot of the Long Man, go left along the Wealdway. At the junction (Waypoint 5) turn left onto the restricted byway to rejoin the route. This will cut the walk to 2.5km (45min).

The Long Man of Wilmington

One of two hill figures of East Sussex, the 72m tall Long Man on Windower Hill is the largest chalk figure depicting a human in Britain. It was probably created in the 16th or 17th century and the original outline only existed as a shadow or indentation in the grass. During restoration work carried out in 1873–74 the outline was marked with whitewashed yellow bricks, which were replaced by breeze blocks in 1969. During WW2 the figure was camouflaged with green paint to avoid it being used by the enemy as a landmark.

The White Horse dominates the views from the river path

WALK 12
Litlington White Horse

Start/finish	*Seven Sisters Country Park Visitor Centre*
Locate	*BN25 4AD ///subtitle.romance.masses*
Cafes/pubs	*Cafe by visitor centre, pub in Litlington and on A259 road near visitor centre*
Transport	*Buses from Brighton and Eastbourne*
Parking	*Visitor centre car park (pay and display)*
Toilets	*At visitor centre*

Time 2¼hr
Distance 7km (4¼ miles)
Climb 160m

A lovely river stroll with views over to an iconic chalk figure of a horse

This easy walk first follows a section of the South Downs Way through woods and then crosses fields to the tiny village of Litlington. There you join the path alongside the snaking Cuckmere River, with one of the two chalk figures of East Sussex dominating the views.

Descending to the village of Litlington

SHORT WALKS SOUTH DOWNS – BRIGHTON, EASTBOURNE AND ARUNDEL

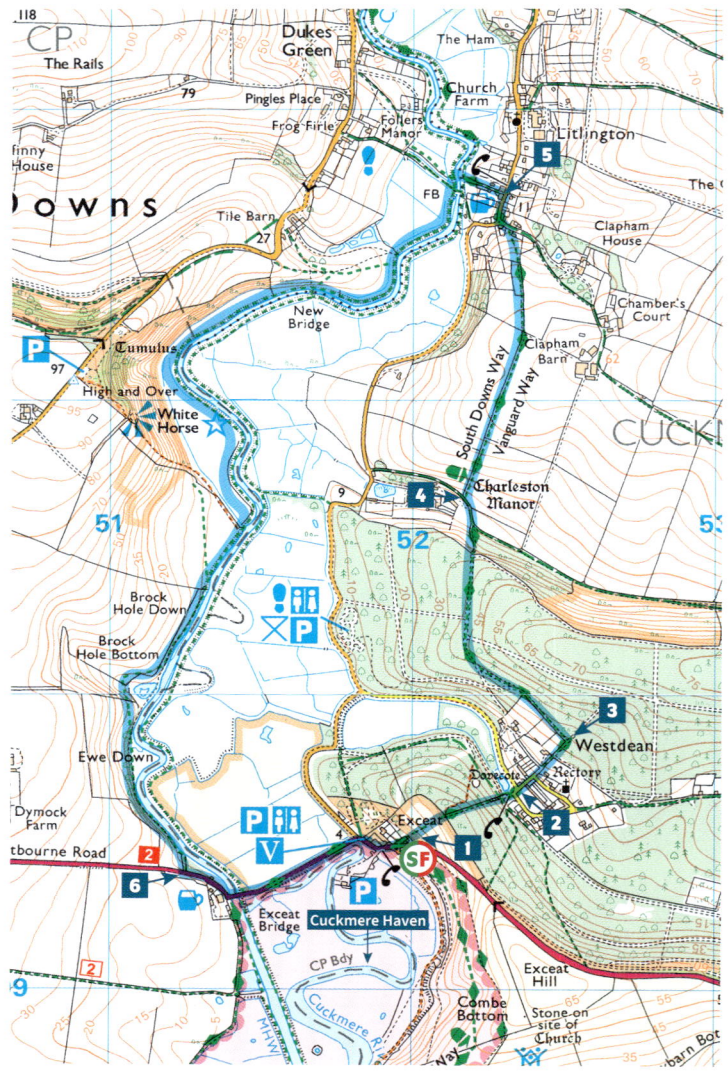

WALK 12 – LITLINGTON WHITE HORSE

1 With the **visitor centre** on your left take the South Downs Way (SDW) towards Alfriston. Go through a gate and walk up the meadow to the low stone wall. Stepping over the wall, follow the SDW through woods. Ignoring other paths, descend the steps to a junction with a lane.

2 Continue straight on along the SDW towards Litlington, with a pond on your left. Passing some cottages in **Westdean**, follow the narrow tarmac lane. When the lane bends right follow the SDW signs left along the track beside a fence, passing further cottages.

3 At the end of the fence keep left on the SDW and follow it for about 15min, occasionally crossing other paths, until you come to a path junction near a house.

4 Keep right along the SDW, crossing over a stile into a field. Head up through the field, with the first views of the White Horse seen on the opposite side of the Cuckmere Valley. Cross a track that runs to a nearby farm. Continue downhill on a path squeezed between grazing fields, going through some kissing gates. On reaching a tarmac lane by a house, go left past **Litlington** village hall. At the road junction go right and just after the pub take the narrow path on the left.

5 This leads to a path junction near the **Cuckmere River**. Keep left along the public footpath (the SDW continues to the right). Shortly afterwards cross a wooden footbridge, go left through a kissing gate and continue with the river on your left. The Cuckmere River is a haven for birds, with kingfisher, redstart, egret and

Follow the Cuckmere River below the White Horse

The Cuckmere Valley is rich in wildlife

lapwing among the many species. Follow the path alongside the river for about an hour, crossing several stiles, with excellent views, first dominated by the **White Horse** on the nearby hillside and then by the river. The path climbs slightly away from the river and arrives at the A259 road.

> **＋ To lengthen**
>
> Upon returning to the visitor centre follow the path down to the beach at Cuckmere Haven and back. This will add about 4km (1hr) to the walk.

6 Turn left and follow the road for about 10min, passing the **Cuckmere Inn** to arrive back at the visitor centre.

The Litlington White Horse

There has been a horse figure on the same site from as early as 1838 or 1860, but the current White Horse was cut in a single night in Feb 1924. The Ministry of Defence covered the White Horse during WW2 to prevent it being used as a landmark. The rush to uncover it after the war left the figure with some changes. In 1949 further changes were made in an effort to restore its original appearance. The site has belonged to the National Trust since 1991 and it is regularly cleaned and maintained by volunteers.

WALK 13
Seaford Head

Start/finish	*Seaford Museum*
Locate	*BN25 1JH ///drill.breaches.wharfs*
Cafes/pubs	*Cafes, restaurants and pubs in Seaford, Cuckmere Inn around halfway*
Transport	*Buses from Brighton or Eastbourne*
Parking	*Esplanade car park*
Toilets	*On the Esplanade near the museum*

Time 3hr
Distance 9.5km (6 miles)
Climb 195m

A scenic walk with uninterrupted views of the iconic Seven Sisters cliffs

Follow the undulating coastal path – with unforgettable views – around Seaford Head to Cuckmere Haven where the river meets the sea. From Cuckmere Haven the route turns inland alongside the river and there is an option to stop at a pub before returning to Seaford.

Clifftop views near the Coastguard Cottages

SHORT WALKS SOUTH DOWNS – BRIGHTON, EASTBOURNE AND ARUNDEL

1 From the **museum** building follow the Esplanade with the sea on your right to the end of the beach. From the Esplanade climb the steps along the England Coast Path and pass the remains of a clifftop house. From 1898 a grand, nine-bedroom colonial-style building stood on the cliff. It was demolished in the 1960s. Follow the well-trodden coastal path, passing Seaford Head **golf course** on your left, and continue for about 20min with more and more views. After a short descent reach **Hope Gap**.

2 Continue along the coastal path, with some amazing views ahead of you of the Seven Sisters cliffs, to reach the Coastguard Cottages.

> Located next to the Coastguard Cottages you can find the remains of Cable Hut 14. From 1918 it housed a cable station for telegraph lines to France. During WW2 the cables running underwater were cut. After the war it was restored and used as a fishing hut.

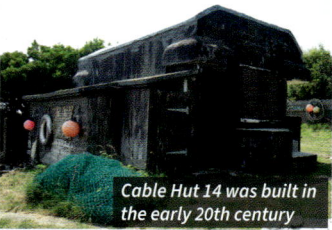

Cable Hut 14 was built in the early 20th century

3 Skirt around the Coastguard Cottages and about 15min from Hope Gap leave the England Coast Path and descend to the pebble beach at **Cuckmere Haven**. Leave the beach on the narrow path by the **Cuckmere River** and follow alongside the river as it bends left. Meet the England Coast Path at a junction.

4 Turn left. The Cuckmere Inn is about 200m to the right if you want to

WALK 13 – SEAFORD HEAD

Approaching Hope Gap with spectacular views of the Seven Sisters

Colourful beach huts in Seaford

stop for refreshment. Ignore a path on the right and look out for a stile on the right that leads to a permissive path over private land.

5 Climb over the stile and go up across the field. Walk beside shrubs, and over a stile to a wide path. Turn right and follow the broad path to **South Hill Barn car park**.

6 Turn left after the barn building, climb over the stile and cross the field to another stile. Reach the coastal path once more, turn right and retrace your steps to **Seaford**.

− To shorten

From Cuckmere Haven return directly to Seaford without taking the path alongside the river. This will reduce the walk to 7km (2hr).

+ To lengthen

When you meet the England Coast Path near the Cuckmere Inn, turn right and walk to the Seven Sisters Visitor Centre. Return to the junction to continue the walk. This will add 2km (30min).

Coastguard Cottages

For centuries this stretch of the coast was a place for smuggling, involving many people from the nearby villages. Built by the navy in 1818, the small cottage housed the officer of the Customs and Excise Watch, and there was also a garrison, home to some armed militia. After the National Coastguard Service was founded in 1822 the cottages became homes for the coastguards and their families. During WW2 Cuckmere Haven was fortified with pillboxes, anti-tank ditches and blocks against invasion and the cottages were commandeered by the army. The cottages are still inhabited today but the buildings are under constant threat due to coastal erosion.

WALK 14
Seven Sisters

Time 4hr
Distance 13km (8 miles)
Climb 490m

A walk along the famous Seven Sisters cliffs with stunning sea views

Start/finish *Seven Sisters Country Park Visitor Centre*
Locate *BN25 4AD ///president.rushed.trainers*
Cafes/pubs *Cafe by visitor centre, cafe at Birling Gap and pub on A259 road near visitor centre*
Transport *Buses from Brighton and Eastbourne*
Parking *Visitor centre car park (pay and display)*
Toilets *By visitor centre and at Birling Gap*

From opposite the Seven Sisters Visitor Centre follow the South Downs Way on the undulating coastal path that runs along the world-famous Seven Sisters cliffs. There's no shortage of scenic views of one of the longest stretches of undeveloped coastline of the south coast. From Birling Gap walk over meadows and then through the Friston Forest before returning to the starting point.

Magnificent views of Birling Gap from the monument on Flagstaff Point

Enjoying the stunning views

WALK 14 — SEVEN SISTERS

1 Go through the gate opposite the **visitor centre** and take the South Downs Way (SDW), which swings slightly left, signed towards Birling Gap. This is a gentle ascent with some nice views of the **Cuckmere River** winding its way towards the sea. Go through another gate, keep right and then drop down to a gate and path junction.

> ⓘ *Sussex has some good locations to search for fossils such as ammonites and remnants of ancient sea creatures preserved in the chalk cliffs.*

2 Cross the paved path through a gate and continue straight on. The SDW curves left (the path straight on leads to the beach). Follow the SDW, rising alongside a fence, and shortly before you reach **Cliff End** you can spot some pillboxes at the end of the beach below.

> During WW2 it was feared that the enemy would try to land on the beach at Cuckmere Haven. Pillboxes were built and anti-tank blocks were installed on the beach and on both banks of Cuckmere River.

3 At the clifftop keep left by the sign towards Birling Gap. Follow the undulating path with views of the iconic white cliffs of the **Seven Sisters**. Shortly after passing Brass Point ignore the path on the left. Pass the William Charles Campbell Monument on **Flagstaff Point** and then further memorials, then go through a gate by the National Trust sign for Went Hill. On reaching a wide path go right and passing some cottages descend to **Birling Gap**. (At low tide you can walk down to the beach).

4 Return to the junction where you met the wide path and continue

Birling Gap

View of the Cuckmere River just before reaching the visitor centre

straight on along the public bridleway. After a gate climb gently up the grassy hillside with the sea behind you. Pass a building and then, keeping beside a line of shrubs, walk across the grazing field with views of **East Dean** on the right. Ignore other paths and walk along the stone wall. Arrive on Crowlink Lane, keep right past a car park and follow the lane to reach Seaford Road (A259) by **Friston Church**.

5 Cross the road and continue onto the yellow public footpath slightly to the left. Go through a gate and keep right, ignoring the path going straight on downhill. Ignore any joining paths and pass a concrete building. Walk alongside a fence, and then descend through ivy-covered trees. Climb over a stile into a field and cross it to a stone wall. Climb over another stile, cross the lane and go up steps to continue on the public footpath. Cross another field to a stone wall, go through a kissing gate and reach a tarmac lane.

6 Turn left and follow this lane for a few minutes as it bends left. Leave the lane to the right on a bike trail opposite Pond Cottage. Ignore any side paths and tracks and carry straight on at every intersection for about 20–30min through **Friston Forest**. Join a gravel road at a bend in **Westdean** and then leave it at a bend as you carry straight on. Go through a gate and follow a track which then becomes tarmac, passing some cottages. Look out for the cylindrical building on the right behind a stone wall. It is a restored 14th-century dovecote. Soon come to a road junction.

7 At the junction turn left on the **South Downs Way** and climb the steps. Ignore other paths and carry straight on over a low stone wall across Cuckmere Meadows and descend to the visitor centre.

> **— To shorten**
>
> At the monument on Flagstaff Point take the path heading inland along Gap Bottom to join Crowlink Lane and reach Friston Church. Follow Waypoint 5 from there. This shortens the route by almost 2.5km (about 45min).
>
> **+ To lengthen**
>
> From Birling Gap continue along the South Downs Way to the Belle Tout Lighthouse and back. This adds an extra 2km (40min).

Seven Sisters

This series of world-famous chalk sea cliffs, separated by the remnants of dry valleys, stretches from the mouth of the Cuckmere River near Seaford to Beachy Head near Eastbourne. With stunning views, the long-distance South Downs Way runs along the clifftops. The white cliffs have featured in many films, including at the beginning of the *Robin Hood: The Prince of Thieves* and at the end of *Atonement*. It also provided a background for a Quidditch World Cup in *Harry Potter and the Goblet of Fire*.

Looking down to Beachy Head Lighthouse

WALK 15
Beachy Head

Start/finish	The Kiosk, Foyle Way, Eastbourne
Locate	BN20 7XL ///mock.apple.stable
Cafes/pubs	Cafes, pubs and restaurants in Eastbourne, The Kiosk at the start, cafe at Beachy Head car park
Transport	Bus from Eastbourne town centre
Parking	Parking along Duke's Drive and King Edward's Parade (B2103)
Toilets	In Helen Garden (about 300m from The Kiosk) and Beachy Head car park

Time 1¾hr
Distance 4.5km (2¾ miles)
Climb 170m

Stunning sea views and the iconic red-and-white striped lighthouse

This short but popular outing from Eastbourne to Beachy Head provides you with endless stunning sea views. The striking red-and-white striped lighthouse dominates the views from the cliffs at Beachy Head.

Looking back down as the path ascends

SHORT WALKS SOUTH DOWNS – BRIGHTON, EASTBOURNE AND ARUNDEL

1 Facing the kiosk on Foyle Way go left on the wide path. Walk alongside the fence with the sea on the left and soon you see the first South Downs Way (SDW) signs. Pass a large grassy sports field and follow the SDW/Wealdway, ignoring other paths, for about 20min with views over the sea. Above Cow Gap when the SDW curves right uphill, make a short detour to the left to get your first glimpse of the Beachy Head Lighthouse.

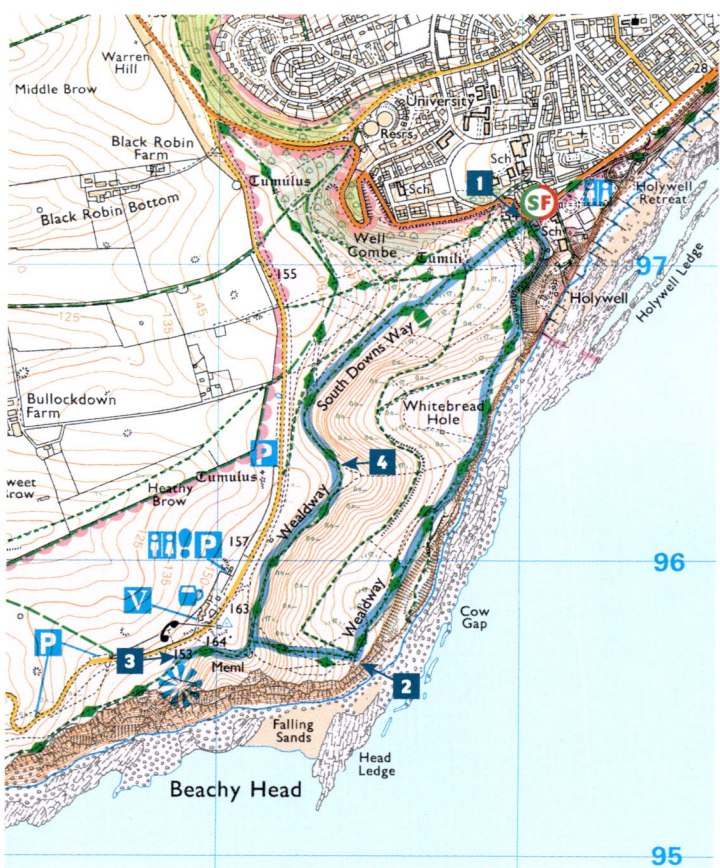

WALK 15 — BEACHY HEAD

View from the coastal path above Cow Gap

2 Continue along the SDW and climb some steps to a small path junction. Keep left on the SDW and shortly afterwards pass a **WW2 memorial** from where there are amazing views of the lighthouse. From the memorial and viewpoint continue along the paved path and near the Beachy Head car park keep slightly left and head to the remains of a watchtower.

3 Just after the watchtower there is a fantastic spot from where you can enjoy the best views of the iconic **Beachy Head Lighthouse**.

Beachy Head Lighthouse was built at the foot of the cliffs in 1902 to replace the nearby Belle Tout Lighthouse. Until 1983 when it was fully automated, lighthouse keepers maintained the revolving light.

From the viewpoint walk back past the Beachy Head car park. Continue along the path roughly parallel to the road with views to the sea and Eastbourne.

4 Shortly afterwards pass a smaller car park (on the other side of the road) and walk to the wooden signpost. Continue along the path signed towards the Seafront and descend back to The Kiosk on the edge of Eastbourne.

View along the coast to Eastbourne

Beachy Head

The name of the highest chalk sea cliff in Britain originates from the word *beauchef*, which means 'beautiful headland'. For centuries it has been a landmark for sailors. This area witnessed some troubled times, from the battle of Portland that took place off Beachy Head in 1653, to a naval engagement in 1690 during the Nine Years War. In 1916 three German U-boats sank 30 merchant ships between Beachy Head and Eddystone, and during WW2 the RAF established a forward relay station to improve communication. In the Cold War, between 1953 and 1957 a radar station operated in the area.

USEFUL INFORMATION

Tourism bodies

South Downs National Park www.southdowns.gov.uk
The National Trust www.nationaltrust.org.uk
Sussex Wildlife Trust www.sussexwildlifetrust.org.uk
English Heritage www.english-heritage.org.uk
Visit South East England www.visitsoutheastengland.com
www.sevensisters.org.uk

Travel

Compass Travel provides bus services throughout East & West Sussex and Surrey. For information and timetables see www.compass-travel.co.uk

Cuckmere Buses operates buses serving local communities in parts of East Sussex not served by commercial bus companies: www.cuckmerebuses.org.uk

See also www.stagecoachbus.com

You can find a useful journey planner at www.buses.co.uk

Attractions

Arundel Castle www.arundelcastle.org
Highdown Gardens www.highdowngardens.co.uk
St Mary's House www.stmarysbramber.co.uk
Bramber Castle www.english-heritage.org.uk/visit/places/bramber-castle
Cissbury Ring www.nationaltrust.org.uk/visit/sussex/cissbury-ring
Devil's Dyke www.nationaltrust.org.uk/visit/sussex/devils-dyke

Clockwise from top: Great views of Cuckmere Haven (Walk 14); A rather attractive waymarker on the South Downs Way; Hope Gap offers great views of the coastline (Walk 13); Chalk grassland and the Cuckmere River (Walk 12)

NOTES

© Nike Werstroh and Jacint Mig 2024
First edition 2024
ISBN: 978 1 78631 203 7

Printed in Turkey by Pelikan Basim using responsibly sourced paper.

A catalogue record for this book is available from the British Library.

© Crown copyright and database rights 2024 OS AC0000810376

All photographs are by the authors unless otherwise stated.

CICERONE

Cicerone Press, Juniper House, Murley Moss, Oxenholme Road, Kendal, Cumbria, LA9 7RL

www.cicerone.co.uk

Updates to this Guide

While every effort is made to ensure the accuracy of guidebooks as they go to print, changes can occur during the lifetime of an edition. Any updates that we know of for this guide will be on the Cicerone website (www.cicerone.co.uk/1203/updates), so please check before planning your trip. We also advise that you check information about transport, accommodation and shops locally. We are always grateful for updates, sent by email to updates@cicerone.co.uk or by post to Cicerone, Juniper House, Murley Moss, Oxenholme Road, Kendal, LA9 7RL.

Register your book: To sign up to receive free updates, special offers and GPX files where available, register your book at www.cicerone.co.uk.